PORTALS OF PEN AND PALETTE

M. Joan Chard

2025

In loving memory

of

my parents and sister

Serial Number: E2546100256
Title: PORTALS OF PEN AND PALETTE
Author: M. Joan Chard
Layout: Merry Oskooei
ISBN: 978-1-77892-231-2
Subject: Poetry, Art
Book format/Size: Royal, Paperback
Pages: 114
Publication Date: August 2025
Publisher: Kidsocado Publishing House

Copyright © 2025 By Kidsocado Publishing House
All Rights Reserved, including the right of reproduction in whole or in part in any form.

Kidsocado Publishing House
Vancouver, Canada

Phone: +1 (236) 333-7248
WhatsApp: +1 (236) 333-7248
Email: info@kidsocado.com
Website: https://kidsocado.com
Address: 2100-1055 West Georgia St,
Vancouver, BC V6E 3P3, Canada

Contents

Part 1: Poems of Inner and Outer Landscape

TO LIFE!	10
AT THE NEW YEAR	12
SPRING IN VANCOUVER	13
TO A BUDDING CHERRY TREE	14
A PLUM TREE OF JAPAN	15
A RHODODENDRON RHAPSODY	17
ELEGY	18
TEA CEREMONY	19
STIR-FRY	22
THRESHOLDS	24
ON WINGS OF LOVE	25
SISTER MOON	26
LOVE'S FULL TIDE	27
FOR A FRIEND	28
MY PIANO'S MEMOIR	29
JUNCTIONS	34
ADVENT ANGELS	35
ON THE NATIVITY	36
LOVE INCARNATE	37
IN PRAISE OF THE TRINITY	38
THE COMMUNION OF SAINTS	39
JESUS CHRIST, THE LIFE OF THE WORLD	40
PILGRIM PEOPLE	42
A CREDAL PRAYER	44
A RHYMING PRAYER	47
WHY?	49

Part 2: A Heart for Nature

The Twin Sisters and Capilano Lake 52
Savary Island Sentinels 53
Salt Spring Island Sanctuary 54
Snows of Solitude 55
Cherry Blossom — panel 56
Iris — panel 57
B.C. Dogwood — panel 58
Heralds of Spring — panel... 59
Vista of Howe Sound
      left panel..60
      right panel 61
Sakura — folding screen 62
A Flight of Fancy — stretched silk 64
Mount Fuji — stretched silk 65
Birch in Spring 66
Lodge at Diamond Head, Garibaldi 68
Village in Devon 70
The North Shore Lions — *shikishi* 71
Bamboo and Maple Leaves — *shikishi* 72
Autumn Songbird — *shikishi* 73
Persimmons — *shikishi* 74
Dogwood — *shikishi* 75
Persimmons for Picking 76
Scottish Shore.. 78

 The *hanko* (signature stamp) on the paintings in which powdered watercolour mixed with glue is applied to stretched silk fabric, panel, and screen, as well as to *shikishi* (10" x 11" silk or paper board), was designed by my Art instructor in Tokyo as an approximation of my name.

Part 3: Haiku-Inspired Verses

harvest moon peers in	82
I shelter beneath	83
rocks dripping seaweed	84
heron's wings outspread	85
autumn's farewell gift	86
in the bamboo grove	87
golden leaves, falling	88
a drifting cloudlet	89
red maples link arms	90
eagles proudly perch	91
blue jay bough-enthroned	92
figures thickly clad	93
kelp fronds sun-ray lit	94
cirrus clouds forming	95
burnished gold remnants	96
gazing totems stand	97
August in Japan	98
Tottori sand dunes	99
stream of irises	100
Mount Fuji snow-capped	101
shoppers scurry past	102
roof tiles moonlight-kissed	103
hosts of umbrellas	104
through *shoji* I hear	105
Savary Island's	106
pines shelter midden	107
kimono and jeans	108
hydrangea bold blue	109
Highland loch-side croft	110
concrete towers teem	111

Part 1: Poems of Inner and Outer Landscape

To Life!

How often we merely tiptoe
tentatively
in the shallow pools
of creative possibility
instead of plunging playfully
trustingly
into the buoyant depths
of living water
by which we are
embraced
enabled
restored!

TO LIFE!

How often we merely tiptoe
tentatively
in the shallow pools
of creative possibility
instead of plunging playfully
trustingly
into the buoyant depths
of living water
by which we are
embraced
enabled
restored!

AT THE NEW YEAR

My diary opens crisply:
a blank page greets me,
its whiteness pristine
as snow freshly fallen
on untrod path
and birdless bough.

What shall I write?
How many words, such vague vessels
of distilled thought, dream, and experience,
will fill this little book,
one page per day,
by year's end?

Why do I wish to record at all?
Why take pen in hand
and inscribe in outline or in detail
the story of today?
Is it to grasp the transient,
to enshrine with worth each fleeting hour?

My first entry sits boldly on its lines
asserting that a new year has begun:
each moment a gift, each act a response,
an opening or a closing, a song or a sigh,
an unfolding chronicle, a mere episode
in the Supreme Author's vast volumes of wonder and surprise.

SPRING IN VANCOUVER

Streets ablush with cherry blossom,
    the city becomes gentler,
  demurely draped in pink lace.

Breeze-borne wispy veils of petals
    alight to the lilt of spring
    upon the lingering snow.

Startling squalls, ruthless ravagers,
      bestrew sodden *sakura*
  in pallid hue, magic sapped.

Traffic rushes by, heedless that
  beneath relentless wheels lies
an erstwhile bower prime plucked.

TO A BUDDING CHERRY TREE

I look through the lattice
of your awakening branches
etched against the clouds of leaden grey,
arms latent with buds
bursting into bloom
facing in trust
towards the light
in life-restoring rite.

Now, again, upon the world
war's vicious volleys are hurled.
Enmity stalks dark'ning skies
unleashing terror, stifling cries.
Innocence in disbelief
mourns hopes for peace turned to grief,
homes deemed havens thrust
instantly to dregs and dust.

I trace the glistening raindrops
jewelling your quivering leaves
cradling springtime splendour
and glimpse a vision
of petals frail,
too soon to fall
in cascading tears
for human frets and fears.

A PLUM TREE OF JAPAN

Ancient *ume*, torn in two,
here you have stood
in gnarled nobility
a presence precious
to generations beyond count,
your limbs, oft assailed by
quaking earth
shrouding snow
raging gale,
prevailing until the fiercest of typhoons
blasted your hold on life.

Your delicate blossoms
have long heralded spring's approach
with modest manner
and cheerful countenance,
their rounded petals
gently opening
despite wintry winds,
their fragrance
awakening the ground from slumber.

In the garden of a Kyushu home
rooted in nurturing soil
maturing in sun and rain
you have been cherished
as a member of the family,

a reminder of ancestral ties
a comfort in challenge and change.

What or who, I wonder,
planted you centuries ago:
a sea-wafted breeze from China,
origin of your species?
a bird dropping a seed?
a child in *yukata* and *geta*?
a grandmother with bent back
and wrinkled smile?

Your tale we will never hear
but pensively beside you
we kneel
where you have fallen,
your head bowed with age
your spine fragmented
your bestowal of beauty
undefiled.

A RHODODENDRON RHAPSODY

Their mountain home now darkness-doffed,
trees of roses bear their blooms aloft
like tapers all ablaze.

A colour-feast before us lies,
beauty's banquet open to the skies,
as fleeting as our days.

On crimson, mauve, magenta hues,
gently washed in morn's distilling dews,
the flick'ring sunlight plays.

Aglow with opalescent sheen,
floral lamps, ensconced in leafy green,
illumine wooded ways.

From Asian hills to Scotian glens
rhododendrons, praised by poets' pens,
their petal-trumpets raise.

ELEGY

Giant cedars moss-festooned
over whom the winds have crooned
you whose boughs embrace the mist
dripping dew, with manna kissed
you who rise to lofty height
reaching for the northern light
nobly stalwart from of yore
peril-stalked, you'll soar no more.

At your feet behold with dread
dwarfish humans' trundling tread
rash despoilers of the earth
come to gauge your ringèd girth
birdsong deaf, their vision blurred
hearts by profit solely stirred
slayers of the greening force
halt for naught their fateful course.

Sawed and sliced, you're sapped and felled
sages of the forest quelled
severed from your sturdy roots
ne'er to greet your nascent shoots
victors in the march of time
victims of a moment's crime.
Circling ravens shriek in scorn;
gales lament, their sighs forlorn.

TEA CEREMONY

The sliding *shoji* subtly welcomes me
     from one world into another:
     from the cacophony of crowds
     and the coldness of concrete
     to enclosed serenity
     scented by cedar and bamboo,
     a rock-and-pool garden beyond.
The *tokonoma* breathes stillness
     in its unobtrusive simplicity
     of hanging scroll and flower arrangement.

The ritual begins:
     her wordless entrance and bow of obeisance
     herald the ceremony,
     this pre-ordained art of honouring tea.
Merely the medium,
     the celebrant incarnates
     a measured mystique.
She evades my open gaze,
     smiles instead at the neutral *tatami*
     on which we both kneel,
     she with accustomed ease,
     I in foreign pose.
Doll-like, poignantly petite and impassive,
     in centuries-weighted layers of *kimono*
     bound by emblem-embossed *obi*,

      she bears the solemnity of the storied past
      and yet seems as fragile
      as pale pink petals fluttering earthward.
With gentle gestures pin-point precise
      as brush-strokes on rice paper,
        with the reverence of a priestess before a shrine
      she deftly employs the utensils,
      each steeped in significance,
      and prepares to serve the precious infusion.

Extending silken sleeves,
      she offers me the jade-green elixir;
      I accept the porcelain bowl in both hands
      and turn it slowly
      to admire its shape and sheen.
The *matcha* lingers bitterly on my lips,
      its rich density new to my palate.
I long for another *nerikiri*,
      a red-bean confection
      daintily designed as a cherry blossom.

This sacrament of aesthetic harmony
      and gracious hospitality
      ends as it began,
      in hushed reverie.
Robed in histrionic dignity,

>   she has performed her scripted role
>   to perfection.
> I glance at her retreating *tabi*,
>   soundless in mincing gait.
> Through the opaque paper door
>   do I hear the smothered sobs
>   of her silent self?

STIR-FRY

Dinner guests are coming
    and they're vegetarian!
The occasion calls for a stir-fry:
    the oil is sizzling in the pan
    daring the ingredients, sliced and diced,
    to plunge in.
First off the chopping board is the onion,
    translucently thin
    yet proudly pungent.
Next are red and green peppers,
    waxily shiny, once bell-shaped,
    like Christmas ornaments.
Quick to enlist is celery,
    straight and stalky,
    a crunchy character.
Mushrooms then join the fray,
    their caps jaunty
    in earthy mode.
Zucchini slides into the mix,
    pale and mellow,
    not at all operatic.
 Broccoli takes a stronger stance,
    its tightly permed crown
    much more dramatic.

Spinach and chard add a leafy touch,
> dark in hue
> and tart in taste.
A handful of almonds, walnuts, pecans
> and a dash of sauce, Worcestershire or Teriyaki,
> give zest to this piquant culinary palette.
Constant stirring is essential,
> colours and textures complementing each other.

Could the tossing and turning
> of human strife
> be transformed this appealingly
> into a new creation,
> a garden of myriad delights
> inviting everyone starved for concord
> to feast at last
> at a common veggie-table?

THRESHOLDS

Is it a vestigial memory
or a fragile foretaste
of the harmony
for which we were created
when one heart thrills
to the beat of another
and reposes
in its homecoming?

In our quest
of the lost Eden
we balance
on the boundary
between
promise and fulfilment.

ON WINGS OF LOVE

Angels wing their way unheard,
unseen their soft descent,
yet how the souls they touch are stirred
as heaven's veil is rent.

Angels look with gentle eyes
upon us day by day;
befriending us in human guise
they sanctify our way.

Angels always find it fun
their rippling joy to share;
they see through clouds the smiling sun
and chase away our care.

Angels have the secret task
of linking heart with heart;
the hidden ones may don a mask
to ply their mystic art.

Angels planned in sheer delight
to weave your life with mine;
they danced, because it seemed so right,
and sipped celestial wine.

SISTER MOON

I gaze at the moon in the starlit sky
and wonder if sometimes she's asking why,
alone in her velveteen, blue-black bed,
on no tender breast she can lay her head.

Mid glorious gold of the sunset's glow
and deepening hush of the world below
she rises and brightens as she holds sway
before she surrenders to dawning day.

Unfettered by bonds of my mortal race,
unwearied by Time's unrelenting pace,
remote in her nearness, compelled yet free,
she radiates silver on land and sea.

Her journey is friendless; she tarries not;
in Sun's embrace she must never be caught;
for him is the day but for her, the night;
together, though parted, they shed their light.

Her splendour ascending to heaven's dome,
a brilliant canopy over my home,
she smiles so serenely that I can tell
she sees my beloved and all is well.

LOVE'S FULL TIDE

Our steps were light beside the sea;
its ceaseless murmurs beckon me
to tread alone this windswept shore
and gently open Mem'ry's door.

Upon a silent, silv'ry strand
we stroll together, hand in hand,
and watch the clust'ring gannets glide
to sheltered nooks above the tide.

The rising moon our tryst o'ersees,
a dusky dune our bed of ease;
each tender tone, each whispered word
by none but winking stars is heard.

Now you and I, though far apart,
have found our haven of the heart;
the waves that surge towards me here
spill forth your love and bring you near.

FOR A FRIEND

Your eyes meet mine in warm embrace
as they have often done before;
but now within a photo frame
you smile at me; I breathe your name.

Your soul with beauty always dwelt
in realms of Nature, music, art;
that summer day you looked entranced
while round your garden sunbeams danced.

Your eyes were lately full of tears
with thoughts of him you loved and missed;
your dearest one had gone ahead—
a lonely path you had to tread.

We freely shared our hopes and cares;
for us when on our last long walk
a bow of promise after rain
affirmed the journey's not in vain.

"Mourn not for me," I hear you plead,
"recall what links us, heart to heart;
in friendship's ties we see a sign
of Love eternal and divine."

MY PIANO'S MEMOIR

Since your birth I have been important to you
    a familiar piece of furniture—yes—
    but so much more:
    the main means of your family's livelihood
    the focus of entertaining guests
    a stable co-dweller amid changing circumstance
    in short, a friend, ever ready to cheer or console.

I owe my origin to Mason and Risch
    piano manufacturers of Toronto
    who from 1871 to 1950
    created instruments of quality and style.
I was chosen by your father, musician and teacher,
    and for twenty-five years
    I held an honoured position
    in his studio, the living-room
    of your parents' first home.

I remember the touch of your baby hands
    and your squeal of delight
    at my response.
Many were the nights in your childhood
    when you drifted into dreams
    to my melodies.

At an early age you began your journey with me—
    before your foot could reach the pedal
    your fingers discovered the cadences
    of my ivory keys
    as you learned how notes work together
    in scales, chords, arpeggios,
    the building blocks of your developing skill
    tested in exam, festival, recital.
I resonated with your eagerness
    to bring out the best in us both,
    to transmute the score of a composer
    into scintillations of sound.

Your father wisely and lovingly
    mentored
    challenged
    encouraged you
    along the pathway of achievement.
My pulse quickened
    at your lively duets
    and rehearsal of solo sections
    of your favourite Beethoven concerto.

I introduced countless others, like yourself,
    to the magic of music making.
Some readily possessed an aesthetic sensibility
    in tone and technique

      whereas most gradually acquired the poise and polish
      of accomplished pianists.
I could usually tell immediately
      which ones sitting before me
      would continue to seek the muse of harmony
      through dedication and perseverance
      and those who would give up the pursuit
      through lack of genuine appreciation
      disciplined attentiveness
      persistent practice.
Playing the piano is, after all, a reciprocal process:
      the performer must exert the utmost energy
      and pour out the purest passion
      to allow my heart-strings to express themselves
      at their full capacity.

In your family's next home
      I resided in a more spacious studio
      and was joined by an electronic organ
      which initially I resented
      as a technologically innovative
      and orchestrally manipulative upstart;
      soon we formed a congenial partnership
      and found a common purpose
      in enabling young and old
      to explore the rich heritage
      of the piano and organ repertoire.

Even when you lived far away
> you never forgot me
> and I am proud to be the initiator of your avocation
> assuring your perennial pleasure.

Your parents' final abode was large enough
> to accommodate me
> their constant companion
> a link to person and place
> vivid in memory.

You and I graced their leisure
> with tunes that danced again
> as in former days.

You smiled wistfully,
> your mind brimming with images
> of your father's elegant hands
> evoking mystic strains from deep within me
> but now content to tap out rhythms of your making
> and to applaud your renderings
> received as flourishings
> of his life's work.

And now here in your home
      we share a past poignantly present.
I stand in my corner
      on curved and carved legs
      sturdy despite my age
      my mahogany warmly mellow.
I welcome your caress of my time-worn keys
      still powerful
      to soothe or stir the soul
      as only music can.

JUNCTIONS

DISAPPOINTMENT
is a harsh wind
when it first strikes
but on passing
ushers in a zephyr
Faith's words of wisdom
Hope's gentle caress
Love's lavish measure

DISAPPOINTMENT
is a pause
for reflection
a window open to
wider landscapes
illumined pathways
closer companionship
with the journeying Spirit

ADVENT ANGELS

On the eve of Jesus' birth
angels hover near the earth
promised blessings to impart
unto each expectant heart.

Casting off our darkest fears,
clearing ev'ry eye of tears,
heaven's heralds, bathed in light,
chase away the cheerless night.

May the glory never fade
lest the dawning turn to shade;
may we angel voices hear
as we journey through the year!

ON THE NATIVITY

Each dark-dispelling Christmas light,
each selfless deed which gives delight
betokens realms beyond our sight.
Through winter's veil of crystal lace
we glimpse a world transformed by grace
and, Spirit-stilled, know Love's embrace.

Each stirring carol we can sing,
each gift or talent we can bring
is tribute poor for such a king.
The Christ, as helpless infant, lies
in stable stark; like us he cries,
the mighty God in human guise.

Eternal Word, the Way made plain,
Incarnate One, with us remain;
in ev'ry heart take up your reign.
For you we seek; by you we're found;
to you we are forever bound.
Like you we rise; like you we're crowned.

Tune: Nashville

LOVE INCARNATE

All praise to Christ, Emmanuel,
our Lord, who longs with us to dwell!
The long-awaited One is born
and deepest darkness turns to morn.

Within a simple stable stall
the heart of God, laid bare for all,
in human form without our sin,
a new creation ushers in.

His mother kneels with wond'ring gaze
and ponders how, in heaven's ways,
this babe she is so blest to hold
can be the king by seers foretold.

Through tears of joy and tears of pain
a vision comes of loss and gain:
she sees a path of thorns ahead
which he, her child, alone must tread.

His eyes and lips still full of love,
his bearing gentle as a dove,
his arms outstretched upon the tree,
he sheds his blood for you and me.

E'en as she lulls his infant cry
she hears triumphant strains on high:
Messiah's reign will never end—
Hosanna, our Redeemer-Friend!

Tune: Wareham

IN PRAISE OF THE TRINITY

In love the Father, Triune God,
whose name above all names we laud,
created us his own to be,
revealing his divinity.

In love the Son, with costly grace,
atoned for sin in ev'ry race;
he gave himself to set us free,
redeeming our humanity.

In love the Spirit, bending near
to comfort, casting out our fear,
attunes the heart to heaven's key,
restoring Eden's harmony.

To Father, Son, and Spirit, praise!
God's love surrounds us all our days;
the Three-in-One, the One-in-Three,
eternal, holy Trinity.

Tunes: Winchester New
       Puer Nobis Nascitur

THE COMMUNION OF SAINTS

A mystic cloud of witnesses
enfolds the Church at prayer;
unseen, yet near, the saints of God
have borne each cross we bear.

In faith they trod the pilgrim path,
by grace they lived the Way
of truth, of peace, of lasting joy;
they walk with us today.

Their eyes were fixed on Jesus Christ,
their trusted Guide and Goal;
they stayed the course to win the race
that's set before each soul.

In darkness they could trace the light,
in weakness they were strong,
in death they found eternal life,
in bliss they join in song.

The Spirit tunes our inner ear
and wakes our inner eye
to praise with them the One alone
on whom we can rely.

In bonds of love, from age to age,
they witness to our Lord,
who ever lives to intercede
and lead us Home restored.

Tune: Belmont

JESUS CHRIST, THE LIFE OF THE WORLD

"I am the Way of Life,
the Alpha and Omega:
the path from thorns may not be free
but I lead those who follow me."

<u>Refrain:</u>

Jesus Christ, the Life of the world,
Jesus Christ, la Vie du monde.

"I am the Bread of Life
and cup of your salvation:
for you the cross I gladly bear,
with you the crown of glory share."

"I am the Morning Star:
my light dispels the darkness;
to all in grim captivity
my name means precious liberty."

"I am the Word of Truth:
my kingdom is eternal;
I ever live to intercede,
to sanctify your deepest need."

"I am the Risen Lord:
I give you joy abundant;
by grace I come to dwell with you
in covenantal love anew."

Part 1: Poems of Inner and Outer Landscape

JESUS CHRIST, THE LIFE OF THE WORLD

Words and tune: M. Joan Chard

1. "I am the Way of Life, the Alpha and Omega: the path from thorns may not be free but I lead those who follow me."

REFRAIN: Jesus Christ, the Life of the world, Jésus Christ, la Vie du monde.

2. "I am the Bread of Life
   and cup of your salvation:
   for you the cross I gladly bear,
   with you the crown of glory share."

3. "I am the Morning Star:
   my light dispels the darkness;
   to all in grim captivity
   my name means precious liberty."

4. "I am the Word of Truth:
   my kingdom is eternal;
   I ever live to intercede,
   to sanctify your deepest need."

5. "I am the Risen Lord:
   I give you joy abundant;
   by grace I come to dwell with you
   in covenantal love anew."

PILGRIM PEOPLE

God, who leads the pilgrim band
in ev'ry age and ev'ry land,
redeem your people as of old;
reveal your wonders yet untold.

God of grace, be still our guide
mid winds of change and tossing tide;
your Presence seen in cloud and flame
still prompts our trust in your strong name.

God of wisdom, speak, that we
may hear the truth that sets us free;
keep us responsive to your call
to seek your kingdom first of all.

God of life and time and space,
Creator of the human race,
you've journeyed with us in the past;
we know you're with us to the last.

Part 1: Poems of Inner and Outer Landscape

PILGRIM PEOPLE

Words and tune: M. Joan Chard

1. God, who leads the pilgrim band
   in ev'ry age and ev'ry land,
   redeem your people as of old;
   reveal your wonders yet untold.

2. God of grace, be still our guide
   mid winds of change and tossing tide;
   your Presence seen in cloud and flame
   still prompts our trust in your strong name.

3. God of wisdom, speak, that we
   may hear the truth that sets us free;
   keep us responsive to your call
   to seek your kingdom first of all.

4. God of life and time and space,
   Creator of the human race,
   you've journeyed with us in the past;
   we know you're with us to the last.

A CREDAL PRAYER

Lord Jesus,

You came to us, Emmanuel, as an infant born into poverty
    in a land familiar with oppression
you were heralded by angels
    and welcomed by shepherds and seers
you were carried into Egypt as a refugee from the powerful
    who were jealous of your kingship
you returned as the Promised One, a second Moses,
    to usher in the new covenant

    IN LOVE.

You lived as one of us
    maturing within a family
    toiling as a craftsman
    treading dusty roads
    teaching and healing
    surrounded by crowds and solitary in prayer
    companioning with the Twelve
    and entrusting your mission to them
    restoring the divine-human relationship

    IN LOVE.

You were betrayed by one who became impatient
      for earthly evidence of your kingdom
you were abandoned by your chosen ones
      who had pledged to follow you unwaveringly
you were arrested and tortured by the forces
      of religious bigotry and political expediency
you were executed along with criminals
      with words of forgiveness on your lips

      IN LOVE.

But death's gruesome grip could not hold you!
The Resurrected One, you burst the bonds of time and space
      amazing us beyond all imagining
      startling us awake to the depths of your grace
      birthing a new creation
      breathing your Presence into receptive hearts and minds

      IN LOVE.

You ascended into the Everlasting Arms
    from which you had come
    to reveal life in all its fullness
    as our high priest you always intercede for us
    your Spirit indwells us
    and we are yours forever.

We praise you,
    Alpha and Omega,
    Redeemer, Paraclete, Friend,

        IN LOVE.

A RHYMING PRAYER

Creator, Sustainer, Sanctifier,
        Temper with tranquillity
        our manifold activity;
        grace us with humility
        and grant us love's simplicity.

        Pity our fragility
        imbued with mutability;
        wake us from passivity
        and curb intractability.

        Pardon our iniquity
        for we confess complicity;
        free us of duplicity
        and shatter shrill hostility.

        Crush our blind cupidity
        which saps the earth's viridity;
        flood our souls' aridity
        and fill them with felicity.

        Deepen magnanimity
        through your divine benignity;
        gladden our festivity
        and bless us with sublimity.

Why?

One day
the mystery
of every anguished why?
will be unveiled
to reveal
a tapestry
designed and wrought
by the consummate Artist.

Then
I will perceive
how each thread
of my life's sunlight and shadow
has been woven
on the loom
of providential care
and prodigal grace.

WHY?

One day
the mystery
of every anguished Why?
will be unveiled
to reveal
a tapestry
designed and wrought
by the consummate Artist.

Then
I will perceive
how each thread
of my life's sunlight and shadow
has been woven
on the loom
of providential care
and prodigal grace.

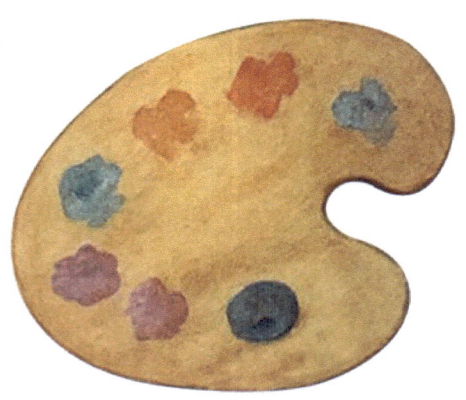

Part 2: A Heart for Nature

The Twin Sisters and Capilano Lake

Part 2: A Heart for Nature

Savary Island Sentinels

Salt Spring Island Sanctuary

Part 2: A Heart for Nature

Snows of Solitude

Cherry Blossom — panel

Iris — panel

B.C. Dogwood — panel

Part 2: A Heart for Nature

Heralds of Spring — panel

Vista of Howe Sound — left panel

Part 2: A Heart for Nature

Vista of Howe Sound — right panel

Sakura — folding screen

Part 2: A Heart for Nature

A Flight of Fancy — stretched silk

Part 2: A Heart for Nature

Mount Fuji — stretched silk

Birch in Spring

Part 2: A Heart for Nature

PORTALS OF PEN AND PALETTE

Lodge at Diamond Head, Garibaldi

Part 2: A Heart for Nature

Village in Devon

Part 2: A Heart for Nature

The North Shore Lions – shikishi

Bamboo and Maple Leaves — shikishi

Part 2: A Heart for Nature

Autumn Songbird — shikishi

Persimmons — shikishi

Part 2: A Heart for Nature

Dogwood — shikishi

Persimmons for Picking

Part 2: A Heart for Nature

The author at an exhibit of her paintings

Scottish Shore

Part 2: A Heart for Nature

俳句

Part 3: Haiku-Inspired Verses

harvest moon peers in—

persimmons in bowl gleam back,

nectar-gushing globes

Part 3: Haiku-Inspired Verses

I shelter beneath

my umbrella shedding tears:

companion in grief

rocks dripping seaweed—

a heron, legs chopsticks-thin,

stabs at wriggling eels

Part 3: Haiku-Inspired Verses

heron's wings outspread—

two fans? or a gingko leaf?

seaside silhouette

autumn's farewell gift:

a ruby-russet carpet

fit for royal tread

Part 3: Haiku-Inspired Verses

in the bamboo grove

quickening shoots inherit

their elders' jade realm

golden leaves, falling,

find rest on a cedar bough—

a fragrant cradle

Part 3: Haiku-Inspired Verses

a drifting cloudlet

kisses sunlit mountain peak

and turns blushing pink

red maples link arms

above the stepping-stoned brook—

I must cross alone

eagles proudly perch

secure in cedar aerie

but still vigilant

blue jay bough-enthroned

squawks o'er autumn's leafy orb—

sapphire set in gold

Part 3: Haiku-Inspired Verses

figures thickly clad

blown atilt by icy blasts

bow to Nature's thrall

kelp fronds sun-ray lit

draw gulls to a seaside feast

spread by hosting waves

Part 3: Haiku-Inspired Verses

cirrus clouds forming

translucent angelic wings—

fragile sign of peace

burnished gold remnants

cling to wind-battered branches:

lamps at winter's door

Part 3: Haiku-Inspired Verses

gazing totems stand

silent mid moss-clad cedars—

slanting darts of rain

August in Japan:

even the wind chime hangs limp—

I dream of ice baths!

Part 3: Haiku-Inspired Verses

Tottori sand dunes

steaming hot beside the sea—

look! there's a camel!

stream of irises,

a garden for the Empress—

rain-bathed purple gems

Part 3: Haiku-Inspired Verses

Mount Fuji snow-capped,

a gigantic ice-cream cone—

quick! soon it will melt

shoppers scurry past

a Buddhist monk statue-still—

snowflakes fill his bowl

Part 3: Haiku-Inspired Verses

roof tiles moonlight-kissed:

the village, harvest-weary,

nestles in silence

hosts of umbrellas,

painted mushrooms on parade,

climb stone steps to shrine

through *shoji* I hear

koto's cooling mountain song

while cicadas hum

Savary Island's

glinting gorse perfumes the shore—

trilling sandpipers

pines shelter midden,

sandy site for feasts of old—

misty scent of clams

kimono and jeans:

age and youth at flower show—

Nature, too, flaunts style!

Part 3: Haiku-Inspired Verses

hydrangea bold blue,

petal circlet its necklace—

goblet for a bee

Highland loch-side croft:

starkly whiter than the sheep

dotting the heathered moor

concrete towers teem

where childhood eyes saw mountains

guarding our green world

About M. Joan Chard:

Born in Vancouver, the author holds degrees from the University of B.C. (B.A.), Dalhousie University (M.A.), Columbia University and Union Theological Seminary (M.A.), and the University of Edinburgh (Ph.D.). She has taught English literature and academic writing in four Canadian and three Japanese universities. In Tokyo she inaugurated courses in Canadian literature and wrote examination material for the Society for Testing English Proficiency.

Her publications include articles on 19th century British fiction, *Japan's Asian Neighbours: A Teacher's Travel Diary* (Tokyo: Kyogaku Sha, 1974), and *Victorian Pilgrimage: Sacred-Secular Dualism in the Novels of Charlotte Brontë, Elizabeth Gaskell, and George Eliot* (New York: Peter Lang, 2019). In addition to writing, her creative activities are in music and painting.

Books by M. Joan Chard:

The Tree that Sat Down
Children's Fiction

A Pony Named Princess
Children's Fiction

Victorian Pilgrimage
(Academic Publication)

www.ingramcontent.com/pod-product-compliance
Lightning Source LLC
Chambersburg PA
CBHW041109070526
44583CB00003B/121